This Book Belongs to:

Sandy Creek
NEW YORK

An Imprint of Sterling Publishing
387 Park Avenue South
New York, NY 10016

Text © 2013 by QEB Publishing, Inc.
Illustrations © 2013 by QEB Publishing, Inc.

This 2013 edition published by Sandy Creek.

Consultant: Fiona Moss, RE Adviser at RE Today Services
Editor: Cathy Jones
Designer: Chris Fraser
Editorial Assistant: Tasha Percy
Design Manager: Anna Lubecka

ISBN 978-1-4351-5239-7

Manufactured in China
Lot #:
10 9 8 7 6 5 4 3 2 1
08/13

The Miracles of Jesus

Written by
Katherine Sully

Illustrated by
Simona Sanfilippo

Sandy Creek
NEW YORK

Jesus loved to teach God's message,
and people loved to listen to him.

They followed him everywhere.

But one day, Jesus was sad because
his cousin, John, had died.

Jesus got on a boat
to rest and pray.

When he came back to shore, the people were still waiting for him.

Jesus welcomed them.

He started to teach and heal the sick people.

All day, Jesus spoke to the crowd.
When evening came, the disciples said to Jesus,
"It's late, and these people are far from home.
Send them away, so they can buy some food."

"You can give them some food," replied Jesus.

"That would cost too much!"
the disciples grumbled.

"Go and find out how much food we have," Jesus told his disciples.

The disciples went off among the crowd. They came back with a boy who had five loaves and two fish.

Jesus told his disciples to sit everyone down in groups. Jesus took the five loaves and two fish and thanked God for the food.

Then he divided the food into baskets
for each of the disciples.

The disciples shared the
food among the people.

Everyone ate as much as they wanted.

CRUNCH!

MUNCH!

YUM!

After everyone had eaten, the disciples collected the baskets.

When they came back, the twelve baskets were full of food!

They couldn't believe their eyes.

Later, Jesus and his disciples went down to the lake. They were going to a town on the other side.

The disciples climbed into the boat. Jesus stayed behind.

"You go on ahead," he told the disciples. "I have something I need to do first."

At last, the crowd went home. Jesus sat alone
on the mountain to pray.

Later that night,
Jesus looked out
over the lake.

SPLASH!

CRASH!

The boat was now far from the shore,
tossing this way and that.
The disciples were struggling to row the boat,
fighting against the wind and the waves.

It was still dark when the disciples saw a white figure coming toward them. They were terrified.

"It's a ghost!" they cried.

But it was Jesus,
walking on the water.

Jesus called to the disciples,
"Be brave! It's only me!"

"Lord, if it's you," Peter replied,
"tell me to come to you on the water."

"Come," Jesus said.

So Peter got out of the boat and
walked on the water toward Jesus.
But he was scared and began to sink.

Jesus held out his hand and caught Peter.
"Did you doubt that God would save you?" Jesus asked.

As they climbed back into the boat,
the wind died down.
The disciples were amazed.

"You really are the Son of God,"
they said to Jesus.

Next Steps

Now that you've read the story . . . what do you remember?

* Why was Jesus sad?
* How many people were in the crowd?
* What food did the disciples find?
* How many baskets of leftovers were there?
* Who walked on the water?
* How did people show they trusted God in the story?

What does the story tell us?
We should trust in God to give us all we need.